First World War
and Army of Occupation
War Diary
France, Belgium and Germany

52 DIVISION
156 Infantry Brigade
Royal Scots (Lothian Regiment)
7th Battalion
1 April 1918 - 3 May 1919

WO95/2897/3

The Naval & Military Press Ltd
www.nmarchive.com
Published in association with The National Archives

Published by

The Naval & Military Press Ltd

Unit 10 Ridgewood Industrial Park,

Uckfield, East Sussex,

TN22 5QE England

Tel: +44 (0) 1825 749494

www.naval-military-press.com

www.nmarchive.com

This diary has been reprinted in facsimile from the original. Any imperfections are inevitably reproduced and the quality may fall short of modern type and cartographic standards.

© Crown Copyright
Images reproduced by permission of The National Archives, London, England, 2015.

Contents

Document type	Place/Title	Date From	Date To
Heading	WO95/2897-3		
Heading	52nd Division 156th Infy Bde 1-7th Bn Royal Scots Regt. Apr 1918-May 1919		
Heading	156th Brigade 52nd Division 1/7th Battalion The Royal Scots Regiment April 1918		
Heading	War Diary Of 1/7th Battalion The Royal Scots From 1st To 30th April 1918 Volume XII		
War Diary	Surafend	01/04/1918	02/04/1918
War Diary	Ludd	03/04/1918	03/04/1918
War Diary	Kantara	04/04/1918	04/04/1918
War Diary	Alexandria	05/04/1918	09/04/1918
War Diary	At Sea	11/04/1918	11/04/1918
War Diary	Marseilles	17/04/1918	17/04/1918
War Diary	St Quentin-En-Tournant	20/04/1918	25/04/1918
War Diary	Mametz	26/04/1918	30/04/1918
Miscellaneous	D.A.G. 3rd Echelon	06/05/1918	06/05/1918
Heading	War Diary Of 1/7th Battalion The Royal Scots From 1st To 31st May 1918 Volume XII		
War Diary	Mametz (Map Hazebrouck 1/100,000)	01/05/1918	07/05/1918
War Diary	Neuville St Vaast (Map Maroeuil 1/20,000)	08/05/1918	23/05/1918
War Diary	T.27.d.3.4 (Maroeuil 1/20,000)	23/05/1918	31/05/1918
Map	Map		
Heading	War Diary Of 1/7th Battalion The Royal Scots From 1st To 30th June 1918 Volume XII		
War Diary		20/06/1918	25/06/1918
War Diary	Mont St Eloy	29/06/1918	29/06/1918
War Diary	T.27.d3.4 Mont St Eloy	02/06/1918	11/06/1918
War Diary	S.23.c.3.4	11/06/1918	19/06/1918
War Diary	T.13.b.4.2	20/06/1918	20/06/1918
Map	Map		
Heading	War Diary Of 1/7th Battalion The Royal Scots From 1st To 31st July 1918 Volume XIII		
War Diary	Mont St Eloy (Map Maroeuil 1/20,000)	01/07/1918	07/07/1918
War Diary	T.27.d.4.5	08/07/1918	20/07/1918
War Diary	Mont St Eloy	21/07/1918	22/07/1918
War Diary	Bois d'Olhain (Map France Sheet 44 B)	22/07/1918	28/07/1918
War Diary	Ecoivres (Map France Sheet 51c)	30/07/1918	30/07/1918
War Diary	B21 A.9.3 (Map France Sheet 51 B)	31/07/1918	31/07/1918
Map	Map		
Heading	War Diary Of 1/7th Battalion The Royal Scots From 1st To 31st August 1918 Volume XIII		
War Diary	Bailleul (Map Bailleul 1/20,000)	01/08/1918	13/08/1918
War Diary	Berles	15/08/1918	20/08/1918
War Diary	Berneville	20/08/1918	20/08/1918
War Diary	Mercatel Area	22/08/1918	23/08/1918
War Diary	Henin	24/08/1918	25/08/1918
War Diary	Heninel	26/08/1918	26/08/1918
War Diary	Fontaine Croisilles	27/08/1918	27/08/1918
War Diary	Mercatel	28/08/1918	30/08/1918
War Diary	Near Croiselles	31/08/1918	31/08/1918

Map	Map		
Heading	War Diary Of 1/7th Battalion The Royal Scots From 1st To 30th September 1918 Volume XIII		
Map	Map		
War Diary	U 13.b and D (Sheet 51 B S.W) U 20.b.4.9	01/09/1918	02/09/1918
War Diary	U.22d.9.4	02/09/1918	02/09/1918
War Diary	U30 D.2.c.8.4 (Sheet 57 C. N.W)	03/09/1918	15/09/1918
War Diary	V.27.a8.5 (Sheet 51 B.S.E)	16/09/1918	18/09/1918
War Diary	D 16b (Sheet 57c NE)	19/09/1918	19/09/1918
War Diary	E19a.3.9 (Sheet 37c N.E)	20/09/1918	24/09/1918
War Diary	D.17.d.4.8 (Sheet 57c N.E) D.13.c.8.6	25/09/1918	26/09/1918
War Diary	D.19.a And B	27/09/1918	27/09/1918
War Diary	Canal Du Nord From Moeuvres-Graincourt Road To E.27.b.6.6	27/09/1918	27/09/1918
War Diary	E.27.b	27/09/1918	30/09/1918
Heading	War Diary Of 1/7th Battalion The Royal Scots From 1st To 31st October 1918 Volume XIV		
War Diary	E.27.b	01/10/1918	01/10/1918
War Diary	L.3.c (Sheet 57c N.E)	01/10/1918	02/10/1918
War Diary	F.30.c And L.6.a	04/10/1918	04/10/1918
War Diary	L.3.C.	05/10/1918	05/10/1918
War Diary	J.3.b	06/10/1918	06/10/1918
War Diary	Izel-Lez Hameau	07/10/1918	18/10/1918
War Diary	Bois De La Haie	19/10/1918	19/10/1918
War Diary	Billy Montigny	20/10/1918	20/10/1918
War Diary	Auby	21/10/1918	23/10/1918
War Diary	Coutiches	24/10/1918	26/10/1918
War Diary	Lecelles	27/10/1918	28/10/1918
War Diary	Mairie Nivelle J.29.c.9.7. (Sheet 44 1/40,000)	28/10/1918	31/10/1918
Heading	War Diary Of 1/7th Battalion The Royal Scots From 1st To 30th November 1918 Volume XIV		
War Diary	Mont Du Proy	01/11/1918	07/11/1918
War Diary	K.22 (Sheet 44 NE)	08/11/1918	09/11/1918
War Diary	Blaton	09/11/1918	10/11/1918
War Diary	Herchies	11/11/1918	26/11/1918
War Diary	Neufvilles	28/11/1918	30/11/1918
Heading	War Diary Of 1/7th Battalion The Royal Scots From 1st To 31st December 1918 Volume XIV		
War Diary	Neufvilles	01/12/1918	31/12/1918
Heading	War Diary Of 1/7th Battalion The Royal Scots From 1st To 31st January 1919 Volume XV		
War Diary	Neufvilles	01/01/1919	31/01/1919
Heading	War Diary Of 1/7th Battalion The Royal Scots From 1st To 28th February 1919 Volume XV		
War Diary	Neufvilles	01/02/1919	28/02/1919
Heading	War Diary 7th Bn Cameronians (Sco Rif) February 1919 Volume XLV		
War Diary		01/02/1919	28/02/1919
Heading	War Diary Of 1/7th Battalion The Royal Scots From 1st To 31st March 1919 Volume XV		
War Diary	Neufvilles	01/03/1919	16/03/1919
War Diary	Soignies	17/03/1919	31/03/1919
Miscellaneous	D.A.G. 3rd Echelon		
Heading	War Diary Of 1/7th Battalion The Royal Scots April 1919 Volume XV		
War Diary	Soignies	01/04/1919	27/04/1919

War Diary   Dunkirk   28/04/1919 03/05/1919

noon/11 (3)

noon/2887 (3)

52ND DIVISION
156TH INFY BDE

1-7TH BN ROYAL SCOTS REGT.

APR 1918-MAY 1919

52ND DIVISION
156TH INFY BDE

156th Brigade.
52nd Division.

1/7th BATTALION

THE ROYAL SCOTS REGIMENT

APRIL 1918.

CONFIDENTIAL.

WAR DIARY

OF

1/7th BATTALION THE ROYAL SCOTS.

From 1st to 30th APRIL 1918.

VOLUME XII.

Army Form C. 2118.

Instructions regarding War Diaries and Intelligence Summaries are contained in F.S. Regs., Part II. and the Staff Manual respectively. Title pages will be prepared in manuscript.

WAR DIARY
or
INTELLIGENCE SUMMARY.   VOLUME XII.

APRIL 1918.

(Erase heading not required.)

Place	1918 Date APRIL	Hour	Summary of Events and Information	Remarks and references to Appendices
SURAFEND	1 - 2		The Battalion prepared to move to Railhead. Transport was returned and the personnel rejoined their companies.	
LUDD	3		The Battalion entrained at LUDD at 1100.	
KANTARA	4		The Battalion arrived at KANTARA EAST at 0200, remaining at No. 1 Base during the day and entraining at KANTARA WEST at 2000. Lt. T.R. BINNIE, 8th Bn., The Royal Scots, and 2/Lt. S. MUNRO, 9th Bn. The Royal Scots, joined the Battalion for duty.	
ALEXANDRIA	5		The Battalion arrived at the docks, ALEXANDRIA, at 0700 and immediately embarked on H.T. "LEASOWE CASTLE".	
	5 - 10		Remained in Alexandria Harbour.	
	8		Captain J. BALLANTYNE rejoined from 2nd Echelon, G.H.Q..	
	9		Major W.T. EWING, D.S.O., rejoined from home leave. 2/Lt. D.J. COSSAR proceeded to No. 1 Base, KANTARA, pending transfer to R.A.F.	
AT SEA	11		Convoy of transports sailed from ALEXANDRIA.	
MARSEILLES	17		Convoy arrived at MARSEILLES about 0900. The Battalion disembarked and entrained at 2100. Captain M. SMITH, M.C., rejoined from hospital. Captain J.C. BELL and Captain J. SCOTT rejoined from MUSTAPHA.	
ST QUENTIN EN TOURMANT	20		After three days' train journey the Battalion arrived at NOYELLES about 0900 and marched to the village of ST. QUENTIN-EN-TOURMANT, where billets were allotted.	
	21 - 24			
	25		Training was carried on, special attention being paid to gas.	

WAR DIARY

INTELLIGENCE SUMMARY.

(Erase heading not required.)

Army Form C. 2118.

APRIL 1918.   VOLUME XII.

Place	Date 1918 APRIL	Hour	Summary of Events and Information	Remarks and references to Appendices
MAMETZ	25		The Battalion, less No. 2 Company, moved at 1115 to RUE entraining there for WIZERNES, which was reached at 0200 on 26th.	WMC
	26	1115	At 1115, the whole Battalion (No. 2 Company having rejoined) marched to billets in MAMETZ, arriving there at 1630.	WMC
	27-30		Training was continued.	WMC
	29		Lt. J. SCOTT left the Battalion to command 156th L.T.M. Battery.	WMC
	30		The Battalion was tested in actual gas and later was lectured on Bayonet Fighting by Lieut.-Col. CAMPBELL, D.S.O.	WMC
			Strength as at 30/4/18:—	
			Officers Other Ranks. With Battalion 38 877 Detached 35 Total 38 912	
			Wm Cowan 2/Lieut., I.O. for O.C. 1/7th Battalion The Royal Scots.	

D. A. G.,
  3rd. Echelon,
    G. H. Q.,
      B. E. F.

    Herewith War Diary of this Unit for the month of April 1918 -
Volume XII.

                                                        Lieut. Col.
       Commanding 1/7th. Battalion The Royal Scots.

CONFIDENTIAL.

WAR DIARY

OF

1/7th BATTALION THE ROYAL SCOTS.

From 1st to 31st May 1918.
VOLUME XII (contd.) with
APPENDIX 28.

Army Form C. 2118

WAR DIARY
INTELLIGENCE SUMMARY
(Erase heading not required.)

VOLUME XII (contd.)

MAY 1918.

Instructions regarding War Diaries and Intelligence Summaries are contained in F.S. Regs., Part II. and the Staff Manual respectively. Title Pages will be prepared in manuscript.

Place	Date 1918 MAY.	Hour	Summary of Events and Information	Remarks and references to Appendices
MAMETZ (Map HAZEBROUCK 1/100,000)	1 - 7		Training continued under company arrangements.	None
	1		Lt. C.E.A. SAUNDERS and 25 O.Rs. were detached for duty with Pioneer Coy. attd. R.E.	None
	7	1430	Nos. 1 and 3 Companies moved to Cavalry Barracks; AIRE.	None
	3		Capt. G.G. WEIR, M.C. rejoined from leave to U.K. and proceeded to 156 Bde. H.Q. as B.T.O.	None
	8	0530	Bn. H.Q., Nos. 2 and 4 Companies moved at 0530 to AIRE. The whole Bn. entrained at 0730 at AIRE and arrived at ACQ about 1330. The Battalion marched to hutments at HILL'S CAMP, NEUVILLE ST VAAST, arriving there at 1830.	
NEUVILLE ST VAAST (Map MARQUION 1/20,000)			Lt. E.T. Smith and 15 O.Rs. attached for duty to 156 L.T.M. Battery.	
	9 -14		Company and Specialist training was continued.	None
	13		Major W.T. EWING, D.S.O., assumed command of the Battalion vice Lt. Col. W.C. PEEBLES, D.S.O., who left Bn. for duty as Divnl. Training Camp Commandant.	None
	15		The 156th Brigade relieved 155th Brigade in the right (WILLERVAL) Section of the Div. Sector. 7th Royal Scots moved into support to the 8th Sco. Rifles and were disposed as follows:- Bn. H.Q., No. 3 Coy. and No. 1 Coy. (less 2 platoons) in HILL'S CAMP, NEUVILLE ST VAAST. 1 platoon, No. 1 Coy., in THELUS POST (A.7.a.) and 1 platoon in COUNT'S WOOD POST (A.6.a.). No. 2 Coy. at T.21.c.9.4. at the disposal of O.C. 1/8th Sco. Rifles. - Half company to hold CANADA trench in event of attack, half company for counter attack as required situated in TOAST trench.	None
	15-22		Bn. H.Q., No. 3 Coy. and 2 platoons No. 1 Coy. carried on with training.	None
	20		Lt. Col. W.C. PEEBLES, D.S.O., proceeded to U.K. to report, in writing, to the War Office.	None
	22.		Lt. R. CAIRNS attached to Bde. HQ. as Gas Adviser.	None
	23		7th Royal Scots relieved 8th Sco. Rifles in the left Sub-Section of the Brigade Section. The Battn. was disposed as under:- No. 2 Coy. on the right, touching up with 4th Royal Scots, from T.28.d.4.5. to T.28.b.8.6. No. 1 Coy. in the centre, from T.28.b.8.6. to T.22.d.9.2. No. 3 Coy. on the left, touching up with 155 Bde. from T.22.d.9.2. to T.22.b.7.7. No. 4	None

Army Form C. 2118.

WAR DIARY
INTELLIGENCE SUMMARY

(Erase heading not required.)

VOLUME XII (contd.) Page 2.

Instructions regarding War Diaries and Intelligence Summaries are contained in F. S. Regs., Part II. and the Staff Manual respectively. Title pages will be prepared in manuscript.

Place	Date 1918 MAY	Hour	Summary of Events and Information	Remarks and references to Appendices
T.27.d.3.4. (MAP 36C NE 1/20,000)	23 (contd.)		No. 4 Coy. in reserve in the BEEHIVE line about T.27.b.central. Bn. H.Q. at T.27.d.3.4. One company 8th Sco. Rifles was attached to protect the left flank of the sub-section and was situated in CANADA trench. Each company in the line had two platoons in the firing line and two in immediate support. See sketch map - Appendix 28.	Wyne
	24-31		During this period the Battn. was engaged in cleaning up and repairing the trenches. At night "No Man's Land" was patrolled. Reconnoitring patrols on several occasions reached the enemy's wire and furnished useful information. Trapping patrols lay in wait for enemy patrols nightly but without success as enemy patrols were very inactive and left the control of "No Man's Land" in our hands.	Wyne
	30		The Corps Commander visited the Battn. trenches.	Wyne
	31		Lt. D.T. McDONALD (7th North'd Fus. attd.) proceeded to U.K. to report in writing to War Office for instructions regarding release from Military Service to resume Medical studies.	Wyne
			The Battn. suffered the following casualties in killed and wounded during the month:- Killed - 3 O.Rs. (2 on 25th and 1 on 30th); Wounded - 2 O.Rs. (1 on 17th and 1 on 26th) The following reinforcements were received - 60 O.Rs. from E.E.F. on 18th. 2/Lt. J.P. TRAYNOR, The Royal Scots, joined for duty on appointment, 21/5/18. Lt. S.J. SPENCE, 9th Royal Scots, joined for duty, 28/5/18. Strength as at 31/5/18:-	Wyne

```
                       O.    O.R.
    With Battn.        28    728
    Detached           12    192
              Total    40    920
```

2nd June 1918.

W.M. Owen 2/Lieut.,

I.O. for O.C. 1/7th Battalion The Royal Scots.

No 1 Coy. from T28b90.55 to T22d85 15
No 2 " " T28d4.5 to T28b90.55
No 3 " " T22d9.2 to T22b77.7 left of Bde Section Bn HQ at T27d34.
No 4 " " T27d4.5 in BEEHIVE Trench in Reserve.
Attached Coy of 1/8 SR situated in CANADA TRENCH.

MAREUIL 1:20,000

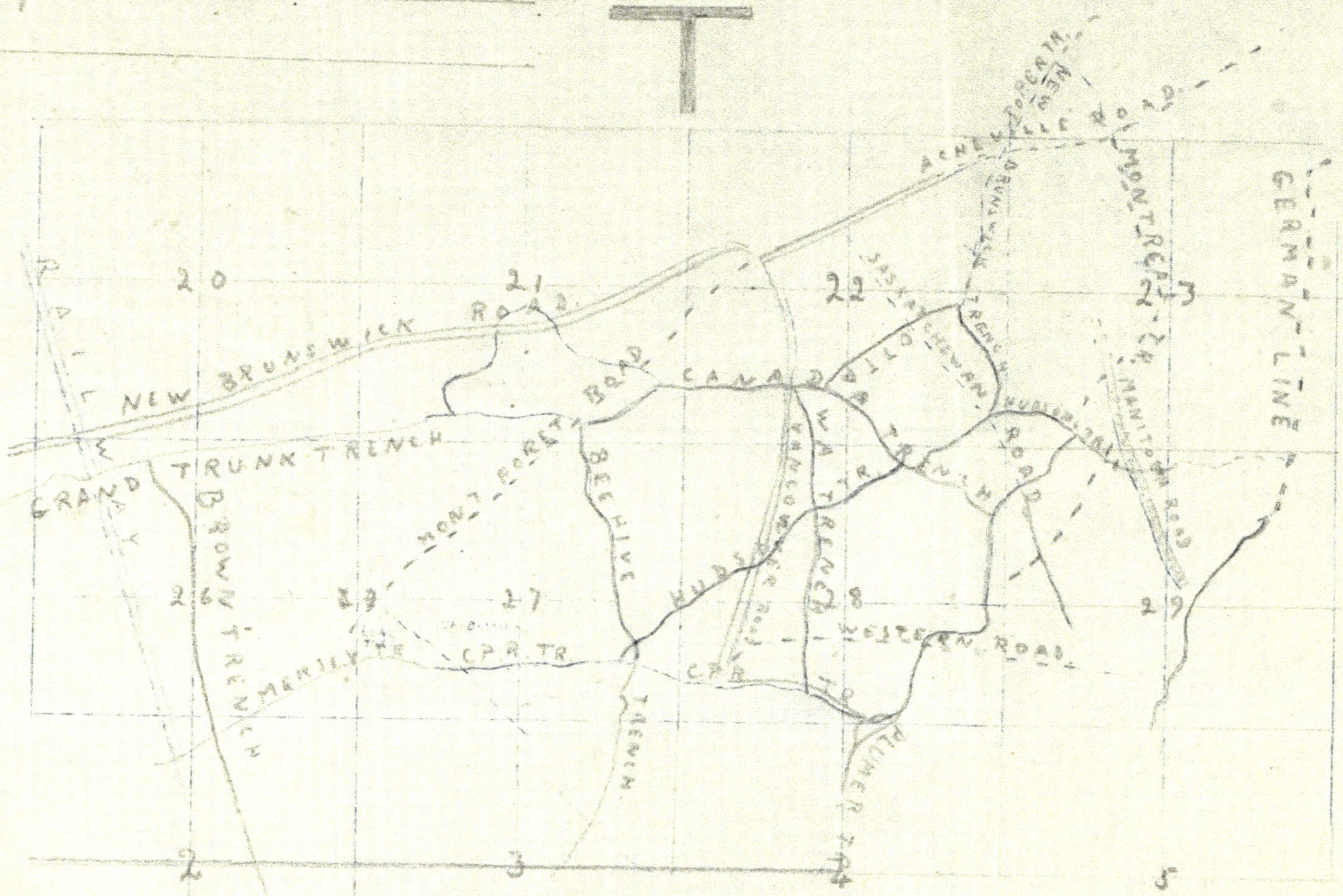

GERMAN LINE
MONTREAL TR
MANITOBA ROAD
ACHEVILLE ROAD
NEW BRUNSWICK ROAD
SASKATCHEWAN
OTTAWA TRENCH
CANADA
BEEHIVE
BEEHIVE TRENCH
VANCOUVER ROAD
HUDSON
WESTERN ROAD
PLUMER TR
CPR TR
MERILY TR
MONT FORET
GRAND TRUNK TRENCH
BROWN TRENCH
RAILWAY
20
21
22
23
26
27
28
29
2
3
4
5

WAR DIARY - 1/7 BATTALION THE ROYAL SCOTS
VOLUME XII APPENDIX 28.

CONFIDENTIAL.

WAR DIARY

OF

1/7th BATTALION THE ROYAL SCOTS.

FROM 1st to 30th JUNE 1918.
VOLUME XII (contd.) with
APPENDIX 29.

Army Form C. 2118.

WAR DIARY
INTELLIGENCE SUMMARY.
(Erase heading not required.)

Instructions regarding War Diaries and Intelligence Summaries are contained in F. S. Regs., Part II. and the Staff Manual respectively. Title pages will be prepared in manuscript.

JUNE 1918.   VOLUME XII (contd.)

Place	Date	Hour	Summary of Events and Information	Remarks and references to Appendices
	1918 June			
	20		Lieut. F.P. MACGILLIVRAY joined Bn for duty from 15th M.G. Battn.	WMcC
	20-29		Wiring and trench repairs were the most important part of the work carried out during this period.	WMcC
	23		Lieut. S.J. SPENCE as O. i/c Patrol of 2 Sections, No. 3 Company, captured two Germans of 46th R.I.R., 119th Divn.	WMcC
	24		2/Lieut. J.G. MACINTOSH appointed Bn Transport Officer vice Lieut. C.M. SMART to hospital. The following officers joined the Bn for duty from U.K.:- Lieut. A.S. MILLER and 2/Lieut. T.S. KILGOUR, 4th R.S.; Lieut. J.C. McCULLOCH, 9th R.S.	WMcC
	25		The disposition of companies was re-organised prior to relief. 2/Lieut. S. MUNRO rejoined from hospital. Lieut. A.S. BILSLAND (Asst. Staff Capt.) cross-posted from 8th Sco. Rifles.	WMcC
MONT ST ELOI	29		The 157th Bde. relieved the 156th Bde. in the left section of the Divisional Sector. On relief by the 6th H.L.I. the 7th R. Scots moved to hutments at FRASER CAMP, MONT ELOI. The Battalion suffered the following casualties in killed and wounded during the month:- 1 O.R. killed 6/6/18. 6 O.Rs. wounded (one of whom died of wounds). During the month notification was received that the following awards had been made:- Major W.T. EWING, D.S.O. Bar to D.S.O. Lt. (A/Capt.) T. McCLELLAND Bar to M.C. 302936, Cpl. (A.L/Sgt.) J. HARVIE M.M. 302909, Cpl. P. CRANE Medaille Militaire. Reinforcements received - 20 O.Rs. on 24/6/18 and 18 O.Rs. on 29/6/18. Strength as at 30/6/18 - O. With Battalion 28 705 Detached 16 181 Total 44 886 Wm McCown 2/Lieut., I.O. for O.C. 1/7th Battn The Royal Scots.	WMcC WMcC WMcC WMcC

Army Form C. 2118.

WAR DIARY

Instructions regarding War Diaries and Intelligence Summaries are contained in F.S. Regs., Part II. and the Staff Manual respectively. Title pages will be prepared in manuscript.

INTELLIGENCE SUMMARY.

(Erase heading not required.)

JUNE 1918.   VOLUME XII (contd.)

Place	1918 June	Hour	Summary of Events and Information	Remarks and references to Appendices
T.27.d.3.4. Mont St Eloy	2	Ref. Map MARQUE 1/20000.	The 157th Brigade relieved 156th Brigade in the right (WILLERVAL) section of the Divisional Sector. The 7th Royal Scots on relief by 6th H.L.I. moved to hutments at FRASER CAMP, MONT ST. ELOY. Captain J.B. GREENSHIELDS, M.C., assumed duty as Second-in-Command of Bn. vice Captain W.R. KERMACK, M.C., to 156th Bde. H.Q.	WMc
	3		The day was devoted to cleaning of billets and equipment.	WMc
	4-10		Company and Specialist training carried out.	WMc
	6		Captain R.A. LENNIE, R.A.M.C.(T.) attached for duty as Medical Officer vice Captain P.J. MOIR, M.C., to hospital.	WMc
S.23.c.3.4.	11		Captain J.C. BELL to hospital. The 156th Brigade relieved the 155th Brigade in the left section of the Divnl. Sector. The 7th Royal Scots relieved the 4th R.S.F. in support to the 8th Sco. Rifles holding the left sub-section. The Battn was disposed as follows:- No. 1 Company in S.18.a. and b. No. 2 Company in BROWN TRENCH S.17. No. 3 Company in JULIA JAMES TRENCH T.14.a. and b. No. 4 Company in PICTOU S.7.a. Bn H.Q. near LA FOLIE FARM S.23.c.3.4.	WMc
	12		Captain J.A. YOUNG to hospital.	WMc
	16		2/Lieut. S. MUNRO to hospital.	WMc
	17		Captain J.C. BELL rejoined from hospital. Lieut. R. CAIRNS rejoined from Brigade H.Q. Lieut. W.S. EVANS proceeded to M.G. Training Centre, GRANTHAM.	WMc
	19		Rev. T.A. STEUART, C.F., joined Bn vice Rev. S.H. SEMPLE, S.C.F., to D.H.Q., 3/6/18.	WMc
T.13.b.4.2.	20		The Battn relieved 8th Sco. Rifles in the front zone, left sub-section, left section of Divnl. Sector. For dispositions see Appendix No. 29. Lieut.	S.E.E. App. 29. WMc

D. D. & L., London, E.C.
(A8001) Wt. W1771/M231. 750,000 3/17 Sch. 82 Forms/C2118/14

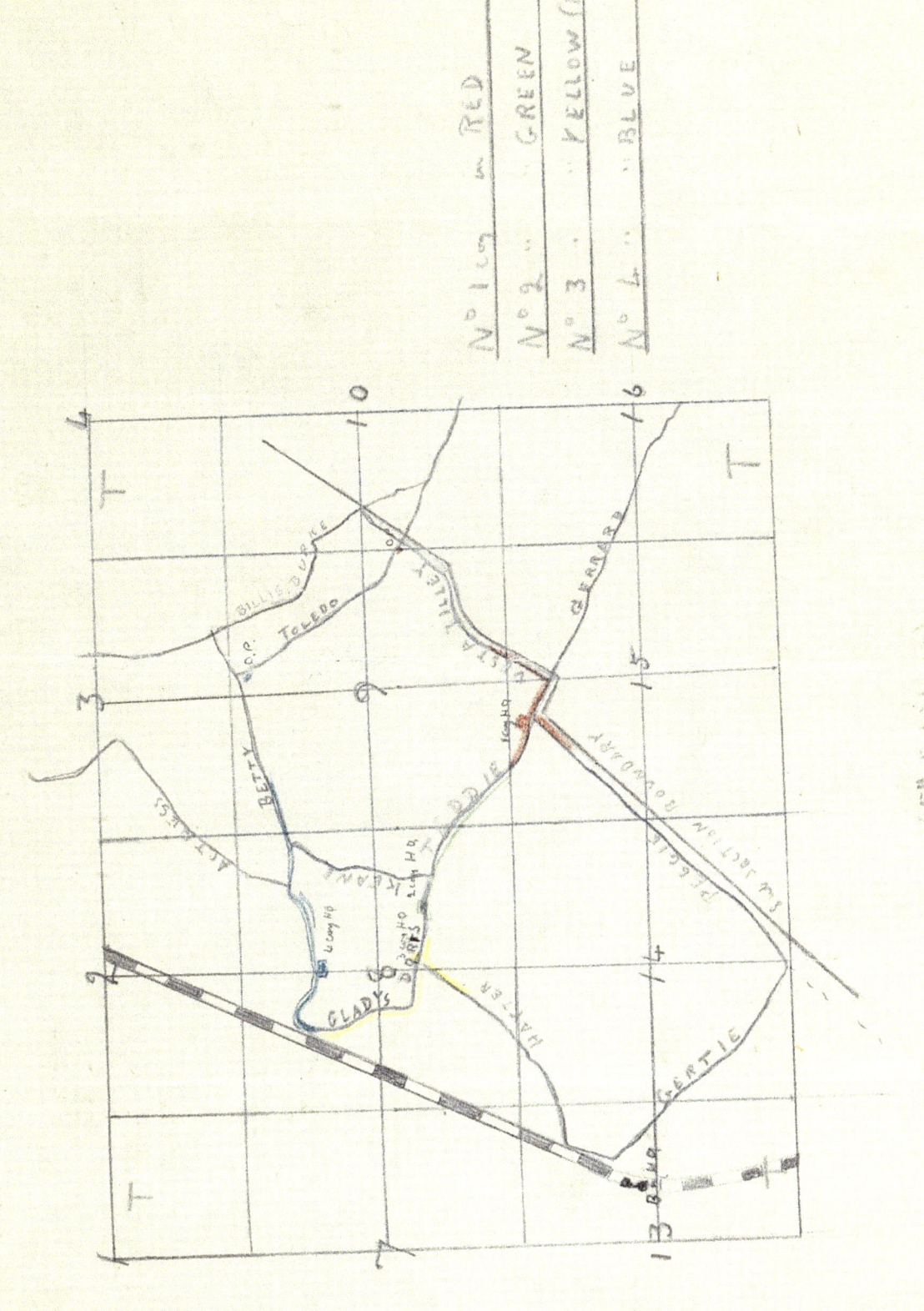

CONFIDENTIAL.

WAR DIARY

OF

1/7th BATTALION THE ROYAL SCOTS.

FROM 1st to 31st JULY 1918.

VOLUME XIII.

Army Form C. 2118.

WAR DIARY VOLUME XIII.

INTELLIGENCE SUMMARY.

(Erase heading not required.)

JULY 1918.

Instructions regarding War Diaries and Intelligence Summaries are contained in F.S. Regs., Part II. and the Staff Manual respectively. Title pages will be prepared in manuscript.

Place	Date 1918 JULY.	Hour	Summary of Events and Information	Remarks and references to Appendices
MONT ST ELOY. (MAP MAROEUIL, 1/20,000)	1		The 156th Brigade was inspected at 10 a.m. by Field Marshal H.R.H. The Duke of Connaught. The Brigade under Lt. Col. J.G.P. Romanes, D.S.O. was drawn up to form three sides of a square. After the Royal Salute had been given, H.R.H. inspected each of the three Battns. Presentation of Decorations followed. The Royal Salute was again given on H.R.H. leaving the parade ground.	None
	2		Captain J. SCOTT left Battn to understudy D.A.D.O.S., 52nd Division.	None
	2-7		Training continued.	None
	7		Brigade Sports were held at Lancaster Camp, MONT ST ELOY. Captain W. HUNTER, 11th R. Scots, joined for duty. G.H.Q. Lists notify the following grants of acting rank:- Major W.T. EWING, D.S.O., to be acting Lieut. Col.; 4/6/18 (List No. 193) Captain J.B. GREENSHIELDS, M.C., to be acting Major, 21/5/18 (List No. 194)	None
T.27.d.4.5	8		The 156th Bde. relieved the 155th Bde. in the Right (WILLERVAL) Section of the Div. Sector: 1/7th The Royal Scots relieved 1/4th R.S.F. in the Left Sub-Section.	None
	9		Lieut. I.M. MOLYNEAUX wounded on patrol: died of wounds on 10th at 42nd C.C.S.	None
	10		Lt. W.F.R. MACARTNEY proceeded on probation to 52nd Bn M.G.C.	None
	8-21 20 21		Work and patrols carried on; no unusual event occurred. 2/Lieut. H.A. SPENCER to hospital. The 8th Div. relieved the 52nd Div. 2nd Bn Devon Regt. relieved 7th R. Scots. The Battn moved to Fraser Camp, MONT ST ELOY.	None None None
MONT ST ELOY.				
BOIS D'OLHAIN (MAP FRANCE, SHEET 44B)	22		The Bde. was inspected by Lt. Gen. Sir AYLMER HUNTER-WESTON, K.C.B., D.S.O. The General shook hands with all ranks who had served under him on GALLIPOLI. Thereafter, the Battn marched to BOIS D'OLHAIN, camping in the wood about Q.14.a. (Map FRANCE, Sheet 44B).	None

Army Form C. 2118.

WAR DIARY VOLUME XIII.

INTELLIGENCE SUMMARY.

(Erase heading not required.)

JULY 1918.

Instructions regarding War Diaries and Intelligence Summaries are contained in F. S. Regs., Part II. and the Staff Manual respectively. Title pages will be prepared in manuscript.

Place	Date 1918 JULY	Hour	Summary of Events and Information	Remarks and references to Appendices
	22 (contd.)		Captain J.A. YOUNG rejoined from sick leave in U.K. Lieut. T.A. HERDMAN, 7th R. Scots, joined for duty.	None
	23 - 29		Training continued.	None
	25		1st Lieut. E.E. GALLAGHER, M.R.C., U.S.A., attached for duty as Medical Officer vice Captain R.A. LENNIE, R.A.M.C.(T.F.) to hospital.	None
	28		Church Parade.	None
ECOIVRES (MAP FRANCE, Sheet 51C)	30		The 156th Bde. marched to the ARRAS district, the 7th R. Scots occupying billets at ECOIVRES.	None
B 21.a.9.3 (MAP FRANCE, Sheet 51B)	31		The 156th Bde. relieved the 11th Canadian Bde.; the 7th R. Scots relieved the 102nd Battn Canadian Infantry in the left Battn front, on the OPPY sector.	None
			The following battle casualties (other ranks) were sustained during the month - Wounded 7: 11th, 14th, 19th and 21st July - one on each day: 18th July - 3. Reinforcements (other ranks) were received as under:- 17 on 5th: 28 on 10th: 17 on 14th: 9 on 24th: 7 on 26th: 2 on 30th 4 on 17th: Total 84.	None
			Notification was received of the award of the following Honours - M.C. Lieut. S.J. SPENCE: M.M. No. 28466, Cpl. H. STANLEY: Mentioned in Despatch from General Sir E.H.H. ALLENBY, G.C.M.G., K.C.B., G.O.C. in C., E.E.F. No. 302936, Cpl. (A.L/Sgt.) J. HARVIE.	None
			Strength as at 31/7/18 - With Bn. O. 24 O.R. 812: Detached O. 21 O.R. 134: With Bn. O. 45 O.R. 946. Total O. 45 O.R. 946.	

W.M. Cowan Lieut.,
I.O. for O.C. 1/7th Battalion The Royal Scots.

2nd July 1918.

CONFIDENTIAL

WAR DIARY

OF

1/7th BATTALION THE ROYAL SCOTS.

FROM 1st to 31st AUGUST 1918.

VOLUME XIII (contd.)

WITH APPENDIX No 30.

WAR DIARY or INTELLIGENCE SUMMARY

Army Form C. 2118.

August 1918. Volume XIII (contd.)

Place	Date 1918 August	Hour	Summary of Events and Information	Remarks and references to Appendices
BAILLEUL (Maj. Bouttel in comd.)	1		Certain changes in the dispositions were carried out which resulted in Nos. 2 & 4 Coys. being in the line with Nos. 1 & 3 Coys. in support. (See Appendix No. 30.)	Wynne
	2.		Captain W.T. Harvey, 7th., Royal Scots, joined for duty.	Wynne
			2/Lieut. J.C. Andrew (4th., R.S.) admitted to hospital, wounded.	Wynne
	4.		Captain K. Mackenzie, (9th, R.S.) joined for duty. Captain J. Bellantyne, admitted to hospital, sick. (8th. H.L.I.)	Wynne
	7		No. 1 Coy. relieved No. 4 Coy., No. 3 Coy. relieved No. 2 Coy. in the front line.	Wynne
			Captain W. Robertson, (16th. R.S.), joined for duty.	Wynne
	9		Captain J. Bellantyne, rejoined from hospital.	Wynne
	13		The Battalion moved into Brigade support on relief by the 1/4th. Battalion The Royal Scots - (for dispositions see Appendix No. 30.)	Wynne
BERLES.	15		The 1/4th. Battalion Gordon Highlanders relieved the 1/7th. Battalion The Royal Scots in Brigade support. On completion of relief the Battalion moved by light railway from ECURIE to billets in and around BERLES (France, Sheet 51cD, F, 8, 14), arriving there about 6 a.m. 16/8/18.	Wynne
	16		Lieut. W.F.R. Macartney, rejoined for duty from 52nd. Machine Gun Battalion.	Wynne
	18-20		Battalion carried on with training.	Wynne
BERNEVILLE	20		The Battalion moved at 11.45 p.m. to BERNEVILLE, (France, Sheet 51c. C6, F1.)	Wynne

Army Form C. 2118.

WAR DIARY
or
INTELLIGENCE SUMMARY.
(Erase heading not required.)

August 1918. VOLUME XIII (contd.)

Instructions regarding War Diaries and Intelligence Summaries are contained in F. S. Regs., Part II. and the Staff Manual respectively. Title pages will be prepared in manuscript.

Place	Date 1918 August	Hour	Summary of Events and Information	Remarks and references to Appendices
MERICOURT AREA	22		The Battalion left BARONVILLE at 2 p.m. by lorries for BRETENCOURT (France, Sheet 51 b, S.W.). At 9 p.m. the Battalion moved out off BRETENCOURT and marched to Brigade assembly point at M 33 d, thence to the front line forming up in depth 200 yards outside the wire from M 36, c, 8, 4, to 8 6, a, 9 6.	none
	23		At 5 a.m. the Battalion advanced with No. 1 Coy. in the front line, No. 2 Coy. as exploiting Company, No. 4 Coy. in support and No. 3 Coy. in reserve. The 1/4th. Battalion The Royal Scots were on our right, the 7th. Battalion Scottish Rifles on our left. Two Tanks operated with the Battalion. The Brigade attack was supported by six Brigades of Field Artillery which put up a magnificient barrage. All objectives were taken without much trouble by 6 a.m. and a line T 1, b 15 to N 31 c 44 was taken up, and consolidated, touching up with the 1/4th. Battalion The Royal Scots on the right and the 7th. Battalion Scottish Rifles on the left. One Officer, 24 other ranks, 3 M.G.'s, 2 T.M.'s and 2 Anti-Tank rifles were captured by the Battalion. This line was maintained all day under H.E. and gas shelling.	none
BINN	24		At 7 a.m. the 1/7th. Battalion The Royal Scots, No. 4 Coy. in front followed by Nos. 2, 1, & 3 Coys., with the 7th. Battalion Scottish Rifles on the left advanced at very short notice and occupied a sunken road from N 32 b 7 6 to N 26 d 5 2 touching up with the 157th. Infantry Brigade on our right. Little opposition was encountered and the objective was gained by 8.10 a.m. During the day the position was heavily shelled with gas and H.E. (24th.-25th.) Patrols were pushed out to the HINDENBURG Line which was found to be well wired and occupied by M.G. detachments.	none
	25		This line was maintained. Enemy artillery was active at intervals during the day and night.	none
HENINEL	26		At 2 p.m. the Battalion concentrated at N 32 b 4 8 and at 7 p.m. moved to CROW TRENCH occupying from N 29 d 3 8 to N 29 d 4 2.	none

Army Form C. 2118.

WAR DIARY or INTELLIGENCE SUMMARY.

(Erase heading not required.)

August 1918. VOLUME XIII (contd.)

Instructions regarding War Diaries and Intelligence Summaries are contained in F. S. Regs., Part II. and the Staff Manual respectively. Title pages will be prepared in manuscript.

Place	Date 1918 August	Hour	Summary of Events and Information	Remarks and references to Appendices
FONTAINE CROISILLES	27		At 10 a.m., the 1/7th. Battalion The Royal Scots with the Canadians on the left and the 1/4th. Battalion The Royal Scots on the right advanced with Nos. 2 & 3 Coys. in front and Nos. 1 & 4 Coys. in the second line. Objective was the road O 11 d 22, North of HENDECOURT. The advance was made under cover of a lifting barrage and supported by Tanks up to the line of the SENSEE RIVER. Little opposition was experienced and the enemy surrendered freely. **2 Officers** (1 Battalion Commander) and **250 other ranks** – 2 – 77 m.m Field Guns – 20 M.G.'s and much material being captured. Heavy M.G. fire at the SENSEE RIVER held up the advance about noon and no further move could be made; the line was formed about O 32 d 14 to O 2 b 22 with the 1/4th. Battalion The Royal Scots on our right covering FONTAINE CROISILLES.	nome
MARCoing	28		At **4 a.m.** the Battalion was relieved by a battalion of the 2nd. Canadian Division and marched into Reserve at M 36 a 27.	nome
	29-30		The Battalion remained in Reserve.	nome
NEAR CROISILLES	31		At 5 p.m. the Battalion moved by march route into support to the battle line about BULLECOURT and HENDECOURT.	nome
			The Battalion suffered the following casualties in killed, died of wounds, wounded, and missing during the month:- Killed, 14 O.R.'s (7 on 23rd. – 2 on 24th. – 5 on 27th.) Died of wounds, 2 O.R.'s (1 on 1/8/18 and 1 on 29/8/18) # Wounded – **8 officers** (Lieut. T. McLauchlan, M.C. on 23/8/18, Lieut. J. McNab (6th. R.S.) on 23/8/18, Lieut. J.C. McCulloch (9th. R.S.) on 27/8/18, Lieut. S.J. Spence, M.C. (9th. R.S.) on 27/8/18, Lieut. C.A. Cole (4th. Yorks) on 23/8/18, 2/Lieut. J.S. Weir (H.L.I.) on 23/8/18, 2/Lieut. D. McLaren (4th. R.S.) or 23/8/18, 2/Lieut. J.C. Arrew (4th. R.S.) or 2/8/18. " 338 O.R.'s (1 on 3/8/18, 2 on 7/8/18, 125 on 23/8/18, 177 on 24/8/18, 6 on 25/8/18, 6 on 26/8/18 and 21 on 27/8/18.) Missing	

Army Form C. 2118.

WAR DIARY
or
INTELLIGENCE SUMMARY.

(Erase heading not required.)

August 1918.   VOLUME XIII (contd.)

Instructions regarding War Diaries and Intelligence Summaries are contained in F. S. Regs., Part II. and the Staff Manual respectively. Title pages will be prepared in manuscript.

Place	Date 1918 August	Hour	Summary of Events and Information	Remarks and references to Appendices
			The Battalion suffered the following casualties in killed, died of wounds, wounded and missing during the month./	Appx
			Missing. 1 Officer, 27/8/18 (Captain K. Mackenzie (9th. R.S.) 1 O.R. 23/8/18.	
			✳ Included in these numbers are 2 Officers and 255 O.R.'s who were gassed.	Appx
			The following reinforcements were received:-	
			Captain W.F. Harvey (7th. R.S.) Joined for duty 1/8/18. Captain K. Mackenzie (9th. R.S.) " " " 4/8/18. Captain W. Robertson (16th. R.S.) " " " 7/8/18. 2/Lieut. T.S. Sharp (R.S.) " " " 30/8/18. 2/Lieut. J. Hewthorne (R.S.) " " " 30/8/18.	
			Strength as at 31/8/18. O. O.R. With Battalion 26 318 Detached 14 299 Total 40 617	
	2nd. August 1918.		W.P.M. Conway, Lieut. I.O. for O.C. 1/7th. Battalion The Royal Scots.	

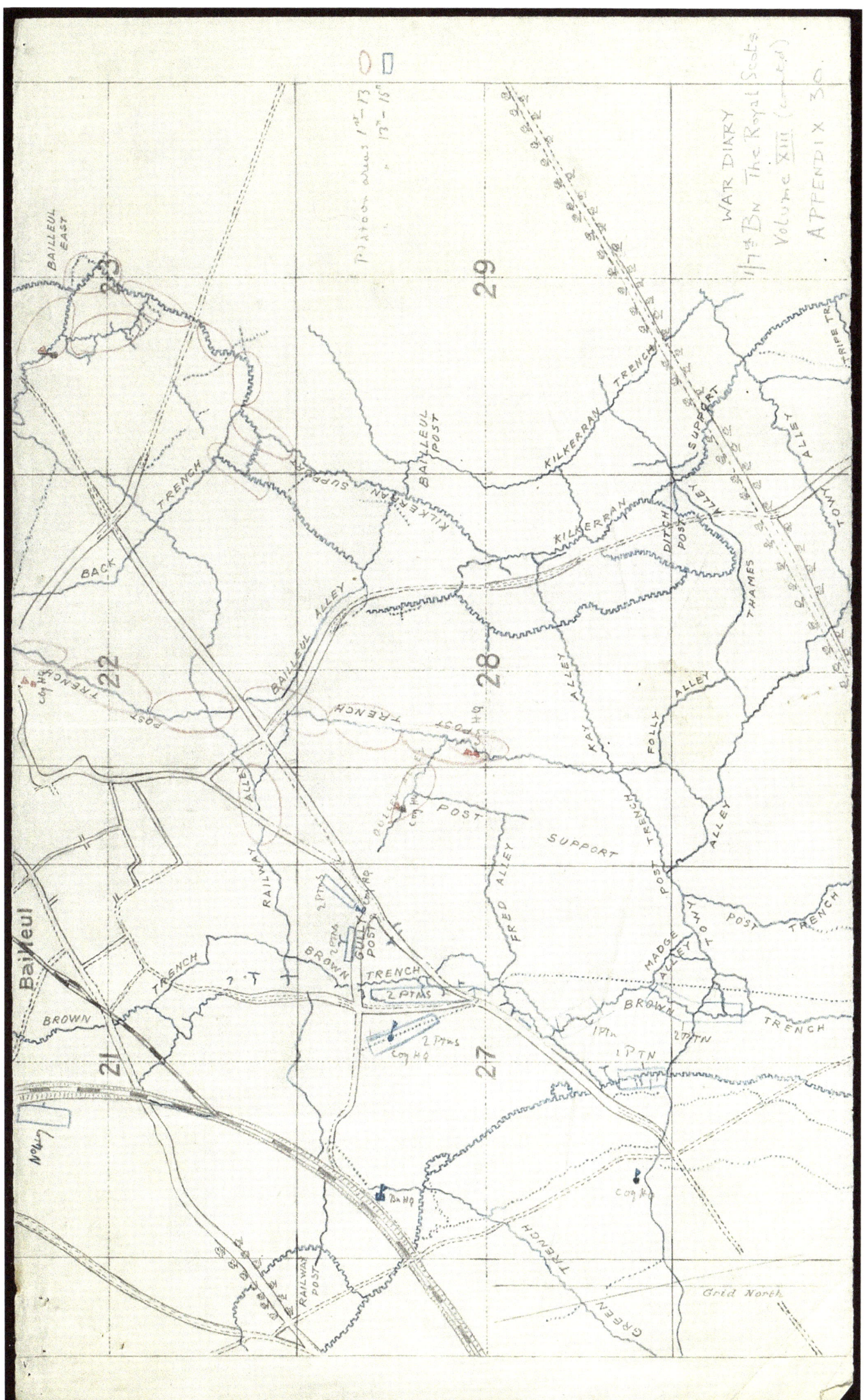

CONFIDENTIAL.

WAR DIARY

OF

1/7th BATTALION THE ROYAL SCOTS.

FROM 1st to 30th SEPTEMBER 1918.

VOLUME XIII (contd.) with

APPENDIX 31.

Army Form C. 2118.

Instructions regarding War Diaries and Intelligence
Summaries are contained in F.S. Regs., Part II.
and the Staff Manual respectively. Title pages
will be prepared in manuscript.

WAR DIARY

SEPTEMBER 1918.   VOLUME XIII (contd.)

INTELLIGENCE SUMMARY

(Erase heading not required.)

Place	Date 1918 SEPT	Hour	Summary of Events and Information	Remarks and references to Appendices
U.20.b. and d (Sheet 51B. S.W.) U.20.b.4.9.	1		**Brigade** The Battalion remained in support all day; the 7th Royal Scots occupied FACTORY AVENUE, U.13.b and d (Sheet 51B. S.W.), moving at 6 p.m. to trenches in U.20.b., with Bn H.Q. at U.20.b.4.9. Nos. 1 and 3 Companies went forward and occupied MARE LANE, relieving two companies of the 1/5th R.S.F. about 8 p.m.	W/Wm.
U.22.d and U.20.b.4.9.	2		The Battalion was in reserve to the Brigade attack on the line D.1.b.3.3. - D.1.b.5.4. - V.25.c.6.1. - U.30.a.9.9. (Sheets 51B. S.W. and S.E. and 57C N.E.). Bn H.Q. and Nos. 1 and 2 Companies moved at 6 a.m. with orders to occupy GORDON RESERVE, U.28.a. (Sheet 51B. S.W.) but before reaching BULLECOURT new orders were received to occupy SELBY LANE and RIPON LANE, U.29.b. (Sheet 51B. S.W.) with Bn H.Q. at U.21.d.2.6. and later at U.22.d.9.4. Companies reached their positions by 11.15 a.m. The Battalion was ordered to roll up the HINDENBURG SUPPORT LINE in V.25 and V.26 as far as a line V.26 central - V.26.d.0.4. (Sheet 51B. S.E.). The order for attack was No. 2 Company as first wave followed by No. 3 Company: No. 1 Company acted as right flank guard, in touch on the right with the 4th Royal Scots: No. 4 Company remained in support in V.25.c. Owing to unavoidable delays, this attack did not develop until 8.30 p.m. No opposition was met and all objectives were reached by midnight.	W/Wm.
U.30.	3	8 a.m.	At 8 a.m. the Bn concentrated at U.30. and remained in this area until the 7th instant.	W/Wm.
B.2.C.8.4 (Sheet 57C N.W.)	7		The Bn moved by march route at 6 a.m. to rest area at B.2.b. (Sheet 51B.S.W. B.2.C.8.4. (Sheet 57C. N.W.)	W/Wm.
	7-15		During this period, three hours daily were devoted to training.	W/Wm.
	12		Captain J.C. BELL proceeded to England to report in writing to the War Office.	W/Wm.
	14		At 9.30 a.m. the Battalion paraded and marched to the Brigade parade ground. At 10 a.m., Lieut. Gen. Sir C. FERGUSSON, Bt. K.C.B., K.C.M.G., M.V.O., D.S.O., Commanding XVII Corps, addressed the 156th Infantry Brigade and congratulated them on the part they had played throughout the recent operations.	W/Wm.
	15			

Army Form C. 2118.

SEPTEMBER 1918. WAR DIARY VOLUME XIII (contd.)

Date 1918 SEPT.	Summary of Events and Information	Remarks and references to Appendices

15	Church parade was held at 11 a.m. At 2 p.m. the Bn paraded and marched to the Brigade parade ground where Major Gen. J. HILL, C.B., D.S.O., Commanding 52nd (Lowland) Division, presented decorations won during the recent fighting. The following Officers, N.C.Os and men of this bn were recipients of awards though not all were at the presentation:-
	MILITARY CROSS - Captain J.C. BELL: Captain J. BALLANTYNE (8th H.L.I. attd.): and Lieutenant J.C. McCULLOCH (9th R. Scots attd.)
	BAR TO THE MILITARY MEDAL - No. 303019, Cpl. J. McROBERTS, M.M.
	MILITARY MEDAL - 300402, L/Cpl. A. STEWART: 301630, Pte. H. GRIERSON:
	    38710, Pte. (A.L/Cpl.) R. BAIRD: 300456, Pte. C. HIGGINS:
	    301603, " R. MORRIS: 275194, Pte. H. KERR:
	    250509, " T. BRYCE: 302896, Sgt. T. RAVIE:
	    302973, " A. MACLEOD: 21118, Pte. A. FUARY:
	     " J. ALEXANDER: 301116, Pte. R. STEENSON.	

16	At 12 noon the Bn paraded in fighting order and marched via ST LEGER - CROISILLES - BULLECOURT to the Reserve Brigade area of the Divnl. sector, relieving the 8th Bn King's (Liverpool Irish) Regt. Relief was complete by 5.30 p.m. Bn H.Q. was situated at V.27.a.8.5., the companies being located in portions of the HINDENBURG LINE, V.27 (Sheet 51B. S.E.).	
18	Lieut. L.R. BINNIE was invalided to England (sick).	
19	The Bn moved at 7.30 p.m. to D.16.b. (Sheet 57C. N.E.) occupying the HINDENBURG LINE trenches in Divnl. Reserve. 2/Lieut. J.P. TRAYNOR (The R. Scots attd.) was admitted to hospital, sick.	
20	At 8 p.m. the Bn relieved the 5th R.S.F. in the right battalion front of the Divnl. Sector: relief was complete by 3 a.m. on the 21st. Dispositions as per Appendix 31.	
21	At 2.50 p.m., a very heavy barrage was brought down on our outpost line and also on the trenches and dug-outs in E.19.a. This barrage gradually crept forward and came to rest on the road in E.20.c. and the trenches parallel to this road, all pill-boxes and dug-outs being directly hit.	

Army Form C. 2118.

SEPTEMBER 1918. WAR DIARY VOLUME XIII (Contd.)

Place	Date	Hour	Summary of Events and Information	Remarks and references to Appendices
	1918 SEPT. 21	(contd.)	The barrage on the front line was extremely heavy, especially on the two northern posts which, it is feared, were annihilated, as none of the garrisons returned. These posts had in the morning suffered severely from trench mortar fire and it is likely that during the attack they must have suffered severely. Everyone "stood to" when the barrage came down and the first sign of an impending attack was the advance of hostile infantry across the roadway in E.20.d.6.2. The infantry were in sections: sections were also seen crawling through the grass. Two S.O.S. rockets were fired when the attack was seen developing. Once the hostile barrage lifted, the posts found themselves attacked with bombs from the front and parties working round their flanks. These parties must have crawled up the saps existing in front of our line, practically under their own barrage. All posts of the outpost line were attacked in the same manner. Hostile Machine Guns were pushed forward with the attack. The platoons retired fighting to a trench in rear, keeping touch with their right: having been reinforced they at once counter-attacked and regained their old position - except at E.20.d.2.6, where a hostile M.G. had gained a position in a pill-box: this was attacked about 5 p.m. and retaken with 2 M.Gs.; 41 Officer and 12 enemy dead were counted in this vicinity). Our old position was regained and a bomb station established. While the platoon posts were fighting on this front, a strong hostile attack was seen approaching between MOEUVRES and our left. This attack was met with fire and counter-attack and repulsed, the enemy retiring. All posts were re-established except the most northern one which it was impossible to approach owing to M.G. fire from E.20.d.6.8. At night it was found necessary to place one platoon 7th Cameronians in the line to enable local supports to be found, for counter-attack purposes. One platoon 7th Cameronians at E.20.a.6.1., two platoons in reserve at E.20.a.4.0., to hold line of resistance and cover any break-through on our left flank.	
		22	The day was on the whole quiet.	
		23	Lieut. E.C. SOMNER was admitted to hospital sick. Enemy	

SEPTEMBER 1918. WAR DIARY VOLUME XIII (contd.) Army Form C. 2118.

INTELLIGENCE SUMMARY.

(Erase heading not required.)

Place	Date 1918 SEPT.	Hour	Summary of Events and Information	Remarks and references to Appendices
	23 (contd.)		Enemy artillery active, but no infantry attack was made on our front.	
	24		The 4th K.O.S.B. relieved the 7th Royal Scots at midnight 23/24th in the right sub-section of the Divnl. sector. The Battn remained under the orders of 155th Infantry Brigade, holding a passive defence line in HORSE LANE and HOBART ST., E.13.c. and 19.a., in event of attack. Bn H.Q. were at D.17.d.4.8. (Sheet 57C. N.E.)	
	25		Bn H.Q. moved up to D.13.c.8.6. 1st Lt. E.E. GALLAGHER, M.R.C., U.S.A., was admitted to hospital sick.	
	26		The Bn remained in the same position. Captain J.M. MORGAN, R.A.M.C., joined for duty as Medical Officer.	
	27		On the evening of the 26th, the Battalion was concentrated in the area D.19.a. and b to be in Reserve to the 156th Infantry Brigade in an attack on the CANAL DU NORD from MOEUVRES - GRAINCOURT ROAD - E.26.b.6.6. - LEOPARD TRENCH, which objectives were to be taken by 1/4th Royal Scots. 1/7th Cameronians were then to pass through 1/4th Royal Scots and make good KANGAROO TRENCH. Preceded by a short and heavy barrage, the attack commenced at 5.30 a.m., 27th Septr., and at 7.15 a.m. the Battalion moved up to the area vacated by 1/7th Cameronians (D.19.b. and b.) who had moved forward behind the 1/4th Royal Scots. At 11.10 a.m. orders were received for the Bn to move forward and consolidate the line of the CANAL DU NORD from MOEUVRES - GRAINCOURT ROAD (inclusive) to E.27.b.6.6. and by 12.15 p.m. the Bn was in position. Information was now received that 1/7th Cameronians were experiencing difficulty with a Machine Gun at E.28.d. and the Bn was ordered up to LION TRENCH (E.27.a.8.1. to MOEUVRES - GRAINCOURT ROAD) to be in support to 1/7th Cameronians and to be ready to help them if called upon. This move was completed by 3 p.m. but the M.G. nest was cleared out without the Bn being called upon as the 63rd Division had passed through. A position of defence in support to the 1/7th Cameronians was taken up in LION TRENCH.	
	28			

Instructions regarding War Diaries and Intelligence Summaries are contained in F.S. Regs. Part II. and the Staff Manual respectively. Title pages will be prepared in manuscript.

WAR DIARY

INTELLIGENCE SUMMARY.
(Erase heading not required.)

Army Form C. 2118.

SEPTEMBER 1918.   **VOLUME XIII (contd.)**   Page 5

Place	Date	Hour	Summary of Events and Information	Remarks and references to Appendices

	1918 SEPT. 28-30		The Bn remained in rest in E.27.b. (Sheet 57C. N.E.).
			
			During the month the following reinforcements were received:-
			
			Captain C.W. SANDERSON and Lieut. E.C. SOMNER joined 8/9/18: 68 O.Rs. on 1/9/18: 29 O.Rs. on 17/9/18: 67 O.Rs. on 25/9/18. Total 2 Offrs. and 164 O.Rs.
			
			Casualties in action were as under:-
			KILLED - Officers - On 21/9/18 - Lieut. T.A. HERDMAN, Lieut. L. MUIRHEAD, and 2/Lieut. R.P. INNES (R. Scots).
			         Other Ranks - 11 on 21/9/18 and 3 on 27/9/18. Total 3 Offrs. and 14 O.Rs.
			WOUNDED - Officers - 21/9/18 - Captain W. ROBERTSON. 27/9/18 - 2/Lt. A.E. WATSON (R. Scots), remaining at duty.
			         Other Ranks - 27 on 21/9/18: 1 on 22/9/18: 2 on 23/9/18: 1 on 25/9/18:
			         1 on 26/9/18: 1 on 26/9/18 (remaining at duty): 6 on 27/9/18:
			         1 on 28/9/18. Total 2 Offrs. and 40 O.Rs.
			MISSING - Officers - On 21/9/18 - Lieut. W.F.R. MACARTNEY (1st Garr. Essex).
			         Other Ranks - 45 on 21/9/18: 4 on 27/9/18. Total 1 Offr. and 49 O.Rs.
			         Total Casualties 6 Offrs. and 103 O.Rs.
			
			Strength of Battalion as at 30/9/18 -
			                               O. O.R.
			        With Battn 21 475
			        Detached 14 190
			        Total 35 665
			
			                      W M Cowan Lieut.,
			               I.O. for O.C. 1/7th Battalion The Royal Scots.
				WWMc
				
				WWMc
				
				WWMc

3/10/18.

CONFIDENTIAL.

WAR DIARY

OF

1/7th BATTALION THE ROYAL SCOTS.

From 1st to 31st October 1918

VOLUME XIV.

Army Form C. 2118.

WAR DIARY VOLUME XIV.
or
INTELLIGENCE SUMMARY.

(Erase heading not required.)

OCTOBER 1918.

Instructions regarding War Diaries and Intelligence Summaries are contained in F.S. Regs., Part II. and the Staff Manual respectively. Title pages will be prepared in manuscript.

Place	Date 1918 OCTR.	Hour	Summary of Events and Information	Remarks and references to Appendices
F.27.B. G.3.C. (and 57C.N.E.)	1		The 52nd (Lowland) Division relieved the 63rd (R.N.) Division in the line S. of CAMBRAI, the 156th Infantry Brigade being in Divisional Reserve. At 1545 the 7th Royal Scots moved to the Reserve Brigade area at L.3.C. (Sheet 57C.N.E.).	WMc WMc
	2		2/Lt. H.A. SPENCER rejoined from sick leave.	WMc
F.30.C. and L.6.A.	4	1930	At 1930 the Battalion moved to the MARCOIGN LINE, E. of the CANAL de L'ESCAULT at F.30.C. and L.6.A. (Sheet 57.C.N.E.) in support to the 157th Infantry Brigade which was holding the line.	WMc
L.3.C.	5	2130	The battalion returned at 2130 to bivouac area in L.3.C. (Sheet 57.C.N.E.).	WMc
J.3.B.	6	0800	The 156th Infantry Brigade moved by march route at 0800 via GRAINCOURT to the BAPAUME-CAMBRAI Road, thence to the vicinity of BOURSIES, where the battalion bivouacked at 1130 in J.3.B. Sheet 57.C.N.E.)	WMc
IZEL-LEZ HAMEAU	7	0930	The Brigade marched at 0930 by LAGNICOURT to the entraining point at VAULX-VRAUCOURT. On arrival at TINCQUES the battalion marched to IZEL-LEZ-HAMEAU arriving in billets at 2100. (Map LENS, 1/100,000).	WMc
	8-10		Cleaning billets and bathing occupied the whole day.	WMc
	10		2/Lt. A.E. WATSON proceeded to England to report in writing to War Office (for tour of duty at home).	WMc
	11		Programme of training was commenced.	WMc
	12		Battn route march during forenoon. At 1330, Lt. Col. JAMES, M.C., of G.H.Q., lectured to Officers, W.Os and N.C.Os on the work of the R.A.F. giving much valuable information regarding the co-operation between infantry and the R.A.F.	WMc
	13		Church parade.	WMc
	14		Training continued. In the afternoon Battn Sports were held. The B.G.C., 156th Infantry Brigade	WMc

Army Form C. 2118.

WAR DIARY
or
INTELLIGENCE SUMMARY.
(Erase heading not required.)

OCTOBER 1918.   **VOLUME XIV.**

Instructions regarding War Diaries and Intelligence Summaries are contained in F. S. Regs., Part II. and the Staff Manual respectively. Title pages will be prepared in manuscript.

Place	Date 1918 OCTR.	Hour	Summary of Events and Information	Remarks and references to Appendices
	14 (contd)		Brigade very kindly presented the prizes to successful competitors at the conclusion of the Sports.	WmC
	15		Route March. Captain W. HUNTER to hospital.	WmC
	16		Training continued.	WmC
	17		Nos. 2 and 3 Coys. carried out a tactical scheme with 156th L.T.M. Battery.	WmC
	18		Training continued. Lieut. E.C. SOMNER rejoined battn from hospital: Lieut. C.A. COLE rejoined from sick leave.	WmC
BOIS DE LA HAIE	19		The 156th Infantry Brigade marched at 0910 from IZEL-LEZ-HAMEAU via AUBIGNY to hutments in BOIS DE LA HAIE, arriving at 1230.	WmC
BILLY MONTIGNY	20		The battalion moved at 0910 by march route via ABLAIN ST NAZAIRE, SOUCHEZ, GIVENCHY, AVION, MERICOURT, to billets at BILLY MONTIGNY, arriving there at 1530.	WmC
AUBY	21		Leaving at 0930 the battalion arrived in billets at AUBY about 1230. (VALENCIENNES, 1/100,000)	WmC
	22-23		Demonstrations were given by the Transport Section and training continued by companies.	WmC
COUTICHES	24		The march was resumed at 0915 via ROOST WARENDIN, WARENDIN, LA PLACHETTE and FLINES to COUTICHES where the battalion occupied billets at 1230.	WmC
	25-26		The battalion was employed on road repairs.	WmC
	27		The battalion left COUTICHES at 0830 and marched to billets in LECELLES arriving there at 1430.	WmC
LECELLES	28		From 1330 onwards the battalion moved off to take over the Divisional Sector from the 5th Royal	WmC

Army Form C. 2118.

WAR DIARY
or
INTELLIGENCE SUMMARY.
(Erase heading not required.)

OCTOBER 1918.   **VOLUME XIV.**

Place	Date 1918 OCTR.	Hour	Summary of Events and Information	Remarks and references to Appendices
MAIRIE NIVELLE J.29.C.9.7. (Sheet 44, 1/40,000)	28 (contd.)		Royal Berks. Regt. Relief was complete by 2130. Nos. 2, 3 and 4 Companies holding the outpost line with No.1 in support. No. 2 Company held CHATEAU L'ABBAYE area J.17.D. No. 3 Company in PETIT MARAIS, J.24.A. No. 4 Company occupied LE LONG BUHOT, K.25.B., each company having two platoon posts and two platoons in support. No. 1 Company were in support in J.30.C. and D.;J.36.A. and B. Battn H.Q. were situated at MAIRIE NIVELLE, J.29.C.9.7. (Sheet 44, 1/40,000).	WMC
	29		Very quiet day. Slight gas shelling at night.	WMC
	30-31		Quiet on the whole with slight enemy shelling and also night harassing fire by his M.Gs.	WMC
			During the month the following reinforcements were received:- 2/Lt. J.A. JAMIESON (6 R.S.) 6/10/18; 2/Lt. J. KERR (7 R.S.) 8/10/18; 2/Lts.D.K.M. GORDON, S.J. CORNFORD, and A. McDOUGALL (4 R.S.) 9/10/18, cross-posted to 1/4 R.S. 11/10/18; 2/Lt. J.W.H. STEUART (R.S.) 9/10/18; 2/Lt. J. CAIRNS (7 R.S.) 13/10/18; Major J. MacD. SMITH (7 R.S.) 28/10/18; 2/Lt. W. GIBB (7 R.S.) 31/10/18. Other ranks - 84 on 2/10/18; 6 on 9/10/18; 2 on 22/10/18; 1 on 26/10/18; 1 on 29/10/18. Total 94.	WMC
			Casualties were as under :- Other Ranks - Killed 1 5/10/18; Wounded 2 5/10/18; 3 30/10/18; 1 31/10/18; Wounded, remaining at duty 1 4/10/18; 1 5/10/18.	WMC

Strength of Battalion as at 31/10/18 -

	O.	O.R.
With Battalion	29	529
Detached	10	261
Total	39	790

W.M. Cowan, Lieut.,
I.O. for O.C. 1/7th Battalion The Royal Scots.

CONFIDENTIAL.

WAR DIARY

OF

1/7th BATTALION THE ROYAL SCOTS.

FROM 1st to 30th NOVEMBER 1918.
VOLUME XIV (contd.)

Army Form C. 2118.

WAR DIARY
or
INTELLIGENCE SUMMARY.   VOLUME XIV.

NOVEMBER 1918.

(Erase heading not required.)

Instructions regarding War Diaries and Intelligence Summaries are contained in F.S. Regs., Part II. and the Staff Manual respectively. Title pages will be prepared in manuscript.

Place	Date 1918 NOVR	Hour	Summary of Events and Information	Remarks and references to Appendices
MONT DU PROY	1		The Battalion was relieved by the 7th Scottish Rifles at 1800 and on relief companies moved into billets, the battalion being in Brigade support; No. 1 Coy. in FRESNOY, No. 2 in NIVELLE, No. 3 in MAIRIE DE NIVELLE, No. 4 Coy. and Bn H.Q. in MONT DU PROY.	WMc
	2 - 7		Three hours training carried out daily.	WMc
K.22. (Sheet 44 NE)	8	1330	The Battalion concentrated at J.22.A. and moved to HERGNIES by the pontoon bridge at K.27.D. From there, the battalion moved forward to the line K.16.central to K.29.central. This line was occupied at 1630 by Nos 1 and 2 Companies, No. 1 Coy. being on the right. Nos 3 and 4 Companies and Bn H.Q. were situated in K.22. (Sheet 44 N.E.)	WMc
	9		Information was received that the enemy had retired East of the ANTOING-POMMEROEUL CANAL and was unlikely to make a stand there, that the VIII Corps Cyclists had gained without opposition the line PERUWELZ-BONSECOURS-LORETTE and that the 157th Inf. Bde. were on the CONDE-PERUWELZ ROAD. The 7th Royal Scots as advanced guard to the 156th Inf. Bde. was ordered to make good the following lines :- (a) CONDE-PERUWELZ Railway between L.7.A.7.5. and L.25.A.9.6., HERGNIES-PERUWELZ ROAD being inter-company boundary inclusive to left company. (b) PERUWELZ-CONDE ROAD, L.3.A.2.7. and L.21.B.7.6., MONT DE PERUWELZ-BONSECOURS ROAD being inter-company boundary inclusive to left company. (c) GADROUILLE-OUTRE L'HAU-LE NOUVEAU MONDE (inclusive to right company)-high ground in L.12.C.-G.19.central; this being the line of the ANTOING-POMMEROEUL CANAL. Nos 3 and 4 Companies forming the vanguard, No. 3 Company on the right, moved from K.22 at 0615 and gained (a), (b) and (c) without opposition, the final line being occupied at 1030. Nos. 1 and 2 Companies with Bn H.Q. moved by road as main guard. The battalion was ordered to concentrate at BLATON and billets were allotted there by 1800. (Sheet 45)	WMc
BLATON	10		The battalion marched at 0930 from BLATON via G.15.C.8.9.-G.17.D.7.8.-14.A.2.3.- HAUTRAGE- SIRAULT, arriving there at 1530. About 1730, the battalion moved to HERCHIES in support to the 7th Scottish Rifles who were attacking the village of ERBAUT which was held by the enemy. This village was successfully cleared by the 7th Scottish Rifles and the 7th Royal Scots	WMc

Army Form C. 2118.

WAR DIARY
or
INTELLIGENCE SUMMARY. VOLUME XIV (contd.)

NOVEMBER 1918.

(Erase heading not required.)

Instructions regarding War Diaries and Intelligence Summaries are contained in F. S. Regs., Part II. and the Staff Manual respectively. Title pages will be prepared in manuscript.

Place	1918 Date NOVR	Hour	Summary of Events and Information	Remarks and references to Appendices
HERCHIES	11		Scots remained overnight in the outskirts of the village. During the early part of the night enemy artillery was active and there were a few casualties in the battalion.	WMc
			By 1100 the news that an armistice had been signed and that hostilities would cease was announced and billets were then occupied in HERCHIES.	WMc
	12-13		Cleaning of kits and billets.	WMc
	14		The Commanding Officer inspected Bn H.Q. and each of the companies separately during the forenoon.	WMc
	15		No. 2 Company paraded at 0630 and marched as part of a representative battalion of the 156th Brigade to MONS, where it lined a portion of the route and later marched past the G. O. C., First Army. This parade commemorated the entry of the British Army into the town.	WMc
	16		Training carried out from 0900 to 1200.	WMc
	17		At 1000, No. 3 Company marched to ERBAUT and represented the battalion at the Divisional Thanksgiving Service. The battalion marched to the Brigade Church Parade at 1400. This parade took the form of a Thanksgiving Service in which the three Chaplains of the Brigade took part. Lt. Col. J.G.P. ROMANES, D.S.O., read the lesson.	WMc
	18		The Commanding Officer inspected the battalion at 1000 in preparation for inspection by B.G.C.	WMc
	19		At 1400 the B.G.C., 156th Infantry Brigade, inspected the 7th Royal Scots. The battalion was drawn up in line with first line transport in rear. After the general salute had been given, the B.G.C. walked round the ranks and inspected the men. While the first line transport was being inspected, the battalion formed up in close column of companies and then marched past the B.G.C., first in ~~line~~ column of companies and then in close column of companies, and thereafter marched back to billets in column of route.	WMc
	20			

Army Form C. 2118.

WAR DIARY
or
INTELLIGENCE SUMMARY.

Instructions regarding War Diaries and Intelligence Summaries are contained in F. S. Regs., Part II. and the Staff Manual respectively. Title pages will be prepared in manuscript.

NOVEMBER 1918. VOLUME XI V (contd.)

(Erase heading not required.)

Place	Date 1918 NOVR	Hour	Summary of Events and Information	Remarks and references to Appendices
	20		2/Lieut. G. STEVENSON, 7th Royal Scots, joined for duty.	Wmc
	22		Lieut. S. MUNRO to hospital.	Wmc
	20-23		Training continued.	Wmc
	23		Capt. W.C. McGEACHIN rejoined from U.K.	Wmc
	24		Church parade was held at 0920. 2/Lieut. R.C. McGLYNN, 4th Royal Scots, joined for duty.	Wmc
	25		The battalion paraded in marching order at 0900 and proceeded on a route march, returning to billets at 1130. Route followed - Road junction C.24.B.5.7. -Cross roads D.22.A.4.9. -ERBAUT-HERCHIES.	Wmc
	26		Inspection of all companies in company drill by 2nd in command of battalion (Major J. B. GREENSHIELDS, M.C.)	Wmc
NEUFVILLES.	28		The battalion moved at 0915 by march route via LENS to NEUFVILLES (near SOIGNIES, Sheet No. 6, BRUSSELS, 1/100,000) arriving in billets at 1300.	Wmc
	29		Cleaning and readjusting billets.	Wmc
	30		ST. ANDREW'S DAY. Observed as a holiday throughout the battalion. 2/Lieut. J.B. ROBERTSON, 7th Royal Scots, joined for duty.	Wmc
			Casualties /	

Army Form C. 2118.

WAR DIARY
or
INTELLIGENCE SUMMARY.

Army Form C. 2118.

Instructions regarding War Diaries and Intelligence Summaries are contained in F. S. Regs., Part II. and the Staff Manual respectively. Title pages will be prepared in manuscript.

NOVEMBER 1918. VOLUME XIV (contd.)

(Erase heading not required.)

Place	Date 1918 NOVR.	Hour	Summary of Events and Information	Remarks and references to Appendices
			Casualties during the month were as under:-	
			WOUNDED - Other Ranks - 1 on 31/10/18 and 4 on 10/11/18.	Appx
			Strength of Battalion as at 30/11/18:-	
			O. O.R.	
			With Battalion 28 710	
			Detached 15 132	
			Total 43 842	
			W. M. Brown Lieut.,	
			I.O. for O.C. 1/7th Battalion The Royal Scots.	

CONFIDENTIAL.

WAR DIARY

OF

1/7th BATTALION THE ROYAL SCOTS.

FROM 1st to 31st DECEMBER 1918.
VOLUME XIV (contd.).

Army Form C. 2118.

WAR DIARY
or
INTELLIGENCE SUMMARY.
(Erase heading not required.)

VOLUME XIV (contd.)

DECEMBER 1918.

Page 1

Instructions regarding War Diaries and Intelligence Summaries are contained in F.S. Regs., Part II. and the Staff Manual respectively. Title pages will be prepared in manuscript.

Place	Date 1918 DECR	Hour	Summary of Events and Information	Remarks and references to Appendices
NEUFVILLES	1	0930	Church Parade.	
	2		Training.	
	3	1000	Ceremonial Parade on Battn Parade Ground. Captain W. HUNTER rejoined from sick leave.	
	4		Training. Major J.B. GREENSHIELDS, M.C., assumed command of the Battalion vice Lt. Col. W. T. EWING, D.S.O., proceeding on leave.	
	5		Training.	
	6	0930	Battalion Route March. Route - NEUFVILLES, MONTIGNIES-LEZ-LENS, LOUVIGNIES, NEUFVILLES. Captain W.F. HARVEY rejoined Bn from duty as Town Major, SIRAULT.	
	7		Training.	
	8	1000	Church Parade.	
	9-12		Training.	
	13		The Divisional Commander, Major Genl. F.J. MARSHALL, C.M.G., D.S.O., inspected the battalion during the forenoon. The battalion was drawn up in close column of companies. After the General Salute had been given, the G.O.C. inspected the companies individually, No. 1 Coy. in rapid wiring and siting strong points, No. 2 Coy. in a tactical scheme, No. 3 Coy. in intensive training à la Brown Book, No. 4 Coy. in company drill.	
	14	0930	Battalion Route March. Route - LOUVIGNIES, MONTIGNIES-LEZ-LENS, NEUFVILLES.	
	15	0930	Church Parade.	
	16-21		Training.	
	17	/		

Army Form C. 2118.

WAR DIARY
INTELLIGENCE SUMMARY.
VOLUME XIV (contd.)

(Erase heading not required.)

DECEMBER 1918.

Place	1918 DECR.	Hour	Summary of Events and Information	Remarks and references to Appendices
	17		Captain C.W. SANDERSON appointed Bn Signalling Officer vice 2/Lt. J. L. PEGGIE, Bn Education Officer.	
	22	1100	Church Parade.	
	23		No. 2 Company was inspected by Brigade Commander (Lt. Col. J.G.P. ROMANES, D.S.O.).	
	24	1000	Battalion Route March. Route - CHAUSSEE N.D., L'HERSE, CHAUSEE ND., NEUFVILLES. 2/Lieut. J.W.H. STEUART to hospital sick.	
	25		Holiday. The Divisional Commander visited the Battalion.	
	26-28		Training.	
	28		The Corps and Divisional Commanders visited the Battalion.	
	29	0930	Church Parade.	
	30		Training.	
	31	1000	Battalion Route March. Route - SOIGNIES, LA RAMEE, BAJENRIEUX, NEUFVILLES. At mid-night, a tattoo parade was held and the New Year brought in.	

			Strength of Battalion as at 31/12/18:- O. O.R.
			                                             With Battalion 24 758
			                                             Detached 17 87
			                                             Total 41 845	

	2nd January 1918.		Lieut. & Asst. Adjt., for O.C. 1/7th Battalion The Royal Scots.	

Confidential

War Diary

of

1/7th Battalion The Royal Scots.

From 1st to 31st January 1919
Volume XV.

Army Form C. 2118.

WAR DIARY
INTELLIGENCE SUMMARY.
(Erase heading not required.)

January 1919. Volume XV

Place	Date 1919 JANY	Hour	Summary of Events and Information	Remarks and references to Appendices
NEUFVILLES	1		In the afternoon the Battalion held a Sports Meeting. The weather cleared for the occasion but on account of heavy rain, going was very heavy.	
	2-4		Training.	
	5		Church Parade was held at 1100.	
	6		The Commanding Officer inspected No 2 and 1 Companies	
	7		Parties Brigade Ceremonial Parade at MONTIGNIES-LEZ-LENS.	
	8		G.O.C., 52nd Division, inspected the Brigade at MONTIGNIES-LEZ-LENS and presented M.M. and M.S.M. ribbons.	
	9-11		Training.	
	12		Church Parade.	
	13-16		Training.	
	17		Brigade practice Ceremonial Parade at MONTIGNIES-LEZ-LENS.	
	18		Divisional Parade on Drill Ground, MAISIERES. The Bun. was drawn up in line of battalions in close column of companies forming three sides of a Square. G.O.C. VIII Corps inspected the Division and presented M.C. and D.C.M. ribbons to L/Cpl's. N.C.O's and men of the Division.	
	19-31		Training.	
	31		Strength of Battalion as at 31-1-19:-	
			With Battalion 22 607	
			Detached 16 196	
			Total 38 803	

Gnd Mather
Lieut & Adjutant,
17th Battn. The Royal Scots.

CONFIDENTIAL.

WAR DIARY

OF

1/7th BATTALION THE ROYAL SCOTS.

FROM 1st. to 28th FEBRUARY 1919.

VOLUME XV (contd.)

Army Form C. 2118.

WAR DIARY or INTELLIGENCE SUMMARY. Volume XV. (contd.)

February 1919.

(Erase heading not required.)

Instructions regarding War Diaries and Intelligence Summaries are contained in F. S. Regs., Part II. and the Staff Manual respectively. Title pages will be prepared in manuscript.

Place	Date	Hour	Summary of Events and Information	Remarks and references to Appendices

NEUFVILLES	1919 Feby. 1-28.		During the month training was carried out under Company arrangements, but was greatly interrupted by the rapid demobilisation of the unit.
			
			Strength of Battalion as at 28/2/19:-
			                      O. O.R.
			With Battalion 17 336
			Detached 10 264
			           Total 27 600
			
			Lieut. & Asst. Adjut.,
			for O.C. 1/7th Battalion The Royal Scots.
			
			2nd. March 1919.	

Army Form C. 2118.

A

Vol 11

WAR DIARY
or
INTELLIGENCE SUMMARY.
(Erase heading not required.)

War Diary.

7th Bn. Camerouians (Sco. Rif.)

February. 1919

Volume XV

Army Form C. 2118.

WAR DIARY
or
INTELLIGENCE SUMMARY.
(Erase heading not required.)

Instructions regarding War Diaries and Intelligence Summaries are contained in F. S. Regs., Part II. and the Staff Manual respectively. Title pages will be prepared in manuscript.

Place	Date	Hour	Summary of Events and Information	Remarks and references to Appendices
Cafe	1/2/19		08.30 - 10.30 Educational Training 10.30 - 12.00 Military training	OM
	2/2/19		Divine Service in Cinema Hall 10.25am	OM
	3/2/19		to Educational Training Instructors A.B.C. Corps. Education in schools Military training 10.30 - 12.00	OM
	4/2/19		08.30 - 10.30 Educational training 11.00 - 12.00 Military Boxing Tournament - al	OM
TARBISE	5/2/19		08.30 - 10.30 Educational. Remainder of day devoted to boxing. Electricity in Cinema Hall	OM
	6/2/19		08.30 - 10.30 Educational Remainder of day devoted training	OM
	7/2/19		08.30 - 10.30 Educational 11.00 - 12.30 Military training. Bar. 79 Competition	OM
	8/2/19		Holiday Semi-Final Div. Football Competition TARBISE 10.30 U73 v 57421. 136 Bde won	OM
	9/2/19		Bde Area Competition completed. B.G.C. Congratulates units	OM
	10/2/19		Divine Service Cinema Hall 11.00	OM
	11/2/19		Route March to ATH.	OM
	12/2/19		08.30 - 10.30 Educational 11.00 - 12.00 Military Training do	OM

WAR DIARY
or
INTELLIGENCE SUMMARY.
(Erase heading not required.)

Army Form C. 2118.

Instructions regarding War Diaries and Intelligence Summaries are contained in F.S. Regs., Part II. and the Staff Manual respectively. Title pages will be prepared in manuscript.

Place	Date	Hour	Summary of Events and Information	Remarks and references to Appendices
	13/2/19		08.30 - 10.30. Educational training. Baking remainder of day	OH
	14/2/19		08.30 - 10.30 Educational 11.00 - 12.00 Military training	OH
	15/2/19		Do	
	16/2/19		8 Offrs. 159 O.R. proceeded from 36th Bn. at Havre for Army of Occupation. Major Sub Williams, Rickie, Thomson, Lieut Julius, Captain Brooks, Harvey Platts & Smith.	
	17/2/19		Educational training suspended owing to lack of instructors and winter use	OH
			Good Duties.	OH
	18/2/19		Cadre of 4 Coys placed under Lieut Thomson for Administration	OH
	19/2/19		Cadres taken into store and cleared old RE	OH
	20/2/19		All available duty men on LO and Brokers.	OH
	21/2/19		Do	OH
	22/2/19		Baking	OH
	23/2/19		Divine Service 11.00. Cinema Hall. R.S.M. Spence left for U.K.	OH
	24/2/19		All available duty men on LO and field Brokers.	OH
	25/2/19		Do.	OH
	26/2/19		Friday. XXII Corps Horse meeting MAZIERRE	OH

WAR DIARY
or
INTELLIGENCE SUMMARY.
(Erase heading not required.)

Army Form C. 2118.

Place	Date	Hour	Summary of Events and Information	Remarks and references to Appendices
	27/2/19		All available men on H.Q. & field sports. 63 O.Rs. have being for 28/2/19 Returns on Japan's Part in the War"	
	28/2/19		All available men on file.	
			During the month an average of 700 men left weekly for Demobilization. On 15/2/19 Staff. 139 O.Rs left for Army of Occupation (A.O.XIX) Transport was maintained at almost full strength. After adhering Great Care & an average of only 10 men were left for duty the Batn. greatly benefited by numerous Educational tours in the surrounding country. The Battalion Cinema was running regularly during the month. One was very acceptable.	

R Blair Lieut Col.
Commdg 1/7 Camerounians

CONFIDENTIAL.

WAR DIARY.

OF

1/7th. BATTALION THE ROYAL SCOTS.

FROM 1st. TO 31st. MARCH 1919.

VOLUME XV. (cont'd)

Army Form C. 2118.

March 1919. WAR DIARY Volume XV (contd.)

INTELLIGENCE SUMMARY.
(Erase heading not required.)

Instructions regarding War Diaries and Intelligence Summaries are contained in F.S. Regs., Part II. and the Staff Manual respectively. Title pages will be prepared in manuscript.

Place	1919 March	Hour	Summary of Events and Information	Remarks and references to Appendices
NEUFVILLES	1 - 9		Training was carried out under Company arrangements.	
	6		Lieut. Col. J.B. Greenshields, M.C., proceeded for demobilisation handing over Command to Captain W. Hunter.	
	11		Draft of 50 O.R.'s proceeded from Mons to join 11th. Battalion The Royal Scots, on the Rhine.	
	13		Captain W. Hunter. promoted Acting Major.	
	16		Draft of 5 officers and 200 O.R.'s proceeded from Mons to join 11th. Battalion The Royal Scots. (Lieut. T.R. Binnie, Lieut. J.G. West, 2/Lieut. R.C. McGlynn, 2/Lieut. H.A. Spencer, 2/Lieut. J.D. Robertson)	
SOIGNIES	17		The Battalion moved by road to Soignies where the 156th. Infantry Brigade was concentrating being now almost reduced to Cadre Strength.	
	18		Battalion reconstituted into one company consisting of the cadre and draft of 10 O.R.'s waiting to join 43rd. Garrison Battalion Royal Fusiliers.	
	19-31		Preparations being made for winding up the Battalion, all stores being checked, Mobilisation Store Table completed, limbers parked. All animals were now sent away.	

Strength of Battalion as at 31/3/19.

	O.	O.R.
With Battalion -	6	60
Detached -	11	31
Total -	17	91

Captain,

Adjt. for O.C. 1/7th. Bn. The Royal Scots.

D.A.G.
　3rd. Echelon,
　　G.H.Q.

　　　　Herewith original copy of War Diary of this unit for April 1919, for disposal please.

　　　　　　　　　　　　　　　　　　　　　Captain,
　　　　　　Adjt. for O.C. 1/7th. Bn. The Royal Scots.

CONFIDENTIAL.

WAR DIARY.

OF

1/7TH. BATTALION THE ROYAL SCOTS.

APRIL 1919.
VOLUME XV (contd.)

Army Form C. 2118.

WAR DIARY VOLUME XV (contd.)
or
INTELLIGENCE SUMMARY.
(Erase heading not required.)

April 1919.

Instructions regarding War Diaries and Intelligence Summaries are contained in F. S. Regs., Part II. and the Staff Manual respectively. Title pages will be prepared in manuscript.

Place	Date April	Hour	Summary of Events and Information	Remarks and references to Appendices
SOIGNIES.	1-26		Battalion occupied in keeping stores and limbers in good condition preparatory to proceeding to U.K.	
	5.		Draft of 10 O.R's proceeded to join 43rd. Garrison Battalion Royal Fusiliers at MARSEILLES.	
	24.		Draft of 8 O.R's proceeded to join 11th. Battalion The Royal Scots on the RHINE, and last men proceeded for demobilization. Battalion now absolutely reduced to Cadre strength.	
	25.		Orders received for the unit to entrain at SOIGNIES on 27th. inst. to move by rail to DUNKIRK, thence to U.K. by sea. Final destination - GAILES.	
	26.		All wagons loaded and final preparations made.	
	27.		Unit entrained with all unit equipment by 1800 along with 4th. Bn. The Royal Scots, and A. & B. Coy's 52nd. Machine Gun Battalion.	
DUNKIRK	28		Unit arrived at DUNKIRK at 1420, train unloaded on quays and stores proceeded to embarkation camp after being kitted and debused	
	29 30		Unit remained in ST POL Camp embarkation being delayed by stormy weather	

Strength as at 30.4.19   Officers   OR
Well R-   4   39
Debused   1   10
                             5   49

Witherinhill Capt
for OC 17th Bn the Royal Scots

(10340) Wt W.5300/P713 750,000 3/18 E 688 Forms/C2118/16

1/7 R Scots Cat **57**

Army Form C. 2118.

WAR DIARY
or
INTELLIGENCE SUMMARY.
(Erase heading not required.)

MAY 1919.

Vol XV (cont.) Jal 14

Place	Date	Hour	Summary of Events and Information	Remarks and references to Appendices
DUNKIRK	2		Awaiting orders for embarkation. All vehicles and stores handed in.	
	3	0900	Bn. 1600 Cadre of Battalion entrained at H.M.T. MOGILEFF at 1200 and next embarked at 1405 from SOUTHAMPTON. Unit embarked 2 Officers 41 O.R.	

on H.M.T. "MOGILEFF"; working party overnight

for Home Establishment.

for O.C. 1/7:Bn The Royal Scots

www.ingramcontent.com/pod-product-compliance
Lightning Source LLC
Chambersburg PA
CBHW081451160426
43193CB00013B/2444